BIBLICAL THEOLOGY AND
THE SOVEREIGNTY OF GOD

T0349126

This Lecture was delivered at
Wesley House, Cambridge, on 21 October 1946,
in commemoration of the twenty-fifth anniversary
of its foundation

Biblical Theology
and
The Sovereignty of God

By

The Rev. LEONARD HODGSON, D.D.

*Regius Professor of Divinity in
the University of Oxford*

CAMBRIDGE
AT THE UNIVERSITY PRESS
1947

CAMBRIDGE
UNIVERSITY PRESS

University Printing House, Cambridge CB2 8BS, United Kingdom

Published in the United States of America by Cambridge University Press, New York

Cambridge University Press is part of the University of Cambridge.

It furthers the University's mission by disseminating knowledge in the pursuit of education, learning and research at the highest international levels of excellence.

www.cambridge.org
Information on this title: www.cambridge.org/9781107649651

© Cambridge University Press 1947

First published 1947
Re-issued 2014

A catalogue record for this publication is available from the British Library

ISBN 978-1-107-64965-1 Paperback

BIBLICAL THEOLOGY AND THE
SOVEREIGNTY OF GOD

I

WE are here to commemorate the foundation of this House, its foundation to be
a home of theological study, twenty-five
years ago. I wonder how many of the young men
who come here as students to-day have any idea
of the mental atmosphere which surrounded their
predecessors a quarter of a century ago. My own
memories go back still further, for I first became
a theological student in 1912, two years before that
August day which marks the great divide, that August
day before which we felt ourselves to be living in
a stable world of orderly progress, after which we
have learned that we live in an unsettled chaos of
catastrophic change. That lesson was not learned all
at once. When peace was signed in 1919 it was hard
to realize that the world we had grown up in was
gone for ever, that neither in politics nor in theology
could we simply pick up the broken threads and go
on where we had left off in 1914. Much of the old
mental atmosphere still survived in the world of
theology when this House was founded in 1921.

As I look back and try to recall what it felt like
to live in that atmosphere, one of my most poignant

memories is of the difficulty we had in thinking of God as truly personal, as personal in the sense of standing over against His created universe, exercising conscious, intelligent control over its development and entering into a relationship of personal intercourse with human beings.

Don't misunderstand me. I am not being so foolish as to suggest that there was ever a time when in the practice of the Christian religion God's character as personal was ignored or forgotten. What I am trying to describe is a period in which the theological student found that his studies tended to make it difficult for him to share in the devotion of his fellow-worshippers in church or chapel, and had this effect by making it difficult for him to think of God as truly personal.

Two factors combined to bring about this situation. The growing influence on thought of the progress of the natural sciences was producing a widespread impression that impersonal laws of nature were the enduring realities underlying the transient experiences and activities of conscious persons. To credit the energy which found expression in the evolutionary process with a consciousness analogous to that of human persons appeared unjustifiable anthropomorphism; it seemed more intelligent to be content, with Matthew Arnold, to speak of 'a power not ourselves making for righteousness', or, with Ralph Waldo Trine, of being 'in tune with the infinite'. To this backwash from scientific progress which flooded the minds of the religious intelligentsia was added the influence of the dominant idealism on the philosophy of religion. The acuteness of the strain upon would-be intelligent Christian believers may be gathered from Sir Walter Moberly's paper on 'God and the Absolute', published in *Foundations* in 1912. He quotes Bernard Bosanquet's rejection of 'the entire doctrine of theism in the Kantian sense, as involving a personal creator and governor of the world'. He quotes Bradley and William James as joining with Bosanquet to celebrate the obsequies of 'the older monarchical theism', and his own contribution is an earnest effort to show that in spite of them all the necessary identification of the God of religion with the Absolute of philosophy need not require the denial of personality in God.

All this evidence, so far, is drawn from before 1914. It is not difficult to prove the continuing influence of the two factors I have mentioned into the nineteen-twenties. Pringle-Pattison's Gifford Lectures were published in 1917, Alexander's in 1927 and William Temple's in 1934. A few quotations from Pringle-Pattison and Alexander will show how they continue Bosanquet's rejection of traditional theism. 'God exists as creatively realizing himself in the world.' 'The divine life is essentially...this process of self-communication. Or, to put it in more abstract philosophical language, the infinite in and through the finite, the finite in and through the infinite—this mutual implication is the ultimate fact of the universe as we know it. It is the eternal fashion of the cosmic Life.'[1] 'God is the whole world as possessing the quality of deity.' 'The body of God is the whole universe and there is no body outside his. For him, therefore, all objects are internal and our minds, therefore, and everything else in the world are "organic sensa" of God. All we are the hunger and thirst, the heart-beats and sweat of God.' 'As actual, God does not possess the quality of deity, but is the universe as tending to that quality.'[2] Alexander, of course, was no Absolute Idealist, and William Temple, too, had gone a long way towards emancipating himself from that philosophy's identification of the life of God with the inner history of the universe. Yet the continued influence of that way of thinking may be seen in his speaking of 'the naïve religious view', calling it 'rather mythological than philosophic', and concluding that to God His creation is 'the means whereby He is eternally that which eternally He is'.[3]

[1] A. S. Pringle-Pattison, *The Idea of God in the Light of Recent Philosophy*, pp. 312, 315.

[2] S. Alexander, *Space, Time and Deity*, Vol. II, pp. 353, 357, 361.

[3] W. Temple, *Nature, Man and God*, pp. 438–9, 495. See also my *Towards a Christian Philosophy*, pp. 159 ff., and *The Doctrine of the Trinity*, pp. 131–4.

When I went to America in 1925 I could feel there the influence of the same mental atmosphere. In that year Kirsopp Lake published *The Religion of Yesterday and To-morrow*. Here he criticized Dean Inge on the ground that having presented 'with conviction and power the case in favour of the ultimate reality of "Values",...instead of saying...that these Values are God, he seems to postulate a God of whom the Values are the attributes'. Lake stated his own position as follows: 'To define God as Purpose, that is the fixed eternal and immutable Laws of the universe, together with the course and results of the evolution which is produced in obedience to them is theology. It is not religion. It becomes religion when it is accepted not as a theory guaranteed by authority, but as an experiment ratified by practice. For the religion of the Experimentalist is primarily the attempt to serve under the Purpose of Life.' The whole aim of prayer, he said, should be to stimulate and quicken the worshipper's aspiration after this Purpose and communion with it: 'I do not believe that the religion of to-morrow will have any more place for Petition than it will have for any other form of magic.'[1]

Just imagine what this mental atmosphere meant for the theological student of those days, the tension produced in his mind by living in a world in which

[1] *Op. cit.* pp. 112, 119, 126.

the would-be religious intelligentsia felt so strongly the pressure of contemporary scientific and philosophical thought that they were ready thus to acquiesce in the dethronement of God from His personal sovereignty. It was well illustrated by an Indian Christian whom I met in New York on my first visit there in 1924. He had just finished two years' post-graduate theological study in America and was about to return to India. He summed up his experience of the Western world by saying that it left him with an inner conflict between his head and his heart. Only from the fundamentalist theologians, whose message his head was unable to accept, could he hear the Word of God which spoke home to his heart.

Many of the utterances of our younger theologians to-day are evidence of the change that has taken place during these last twenty-five years. The clearest evidence is a tendency in some quarters to criticize older theologians with criticisms that reveal the critics to be insensitive to the trials that beset the youth of their seniors. I doubt if many theological students now find Walter Moberly's essay in *Foundations* speak to their condition, or if Moberly himself to-day feels that that essay meets the point at which their challenged faith most needs reinforcement. How has this come about? Although the effects have become apparent within the last twenty-five years, it was, of

course, being prepared for before 1921. The Gifford
Lectures of W. R. Sorley and C. C. J. Webb show
philosophers realizing that man's awareness of standing over against God must be taken more seriously
than had been allowed for in the dominant tradition
of Absolute Idealism. So far as the development of
my own thought is concerned, I shall always remember the work of those two men as having
exercised the chief liberating influence on the purely
intellectual side. I do not suppose I am alone in this;
there must be many others who share my debt to
them. But when one looks beyond the sphere of
purely intellectual argument, I have very little doubt
that the influence which contributed most to the
liberation of the mind and heart and will of intelligent Christianity in this country was that of Baron
von Hügel. I would associate myself with what
Mr P. F. Chambers has recently written in his admirable memoir:

Von Hügel's effort to bring back Christian theology to the prevenience, the 'otherness', the over-
againstness of God, has led some to compare him
with the Swiss theologian Karl Barth, who has done
so much to turn Protestant theology in the same
direction. But Dr John Baillie has probably said the
true thing on this matter: 'Great as is the service
which Dr Barth has rendered us in weaning us from
the enticements of a one-sided immanentism, he has
tended to lead us astray in his apparent complete

rejection of the truth for which immanentism and mysticism alike stand. And probably when the theological excitement of these present years gives place to a period of calmer reflection it will be recognized that Von Hügel was here the safer guide.'[1]

It is time now to sum up the change I have been trying to describe, the change which undoubtedly has come about, whoever or whatever may have produced it. Let me put it like this. Theologians no longer feel it necessary to apologize for thinking and speaking of God as the sovereign personal creator, ruler, redeemer and judge of this time-space universe, as having given to His creation a relative freedom and independence so that He stands over against it in personal relations. They no longer regard such ways of thinking and speaking as the expression of 'the naïve religious view...rather mythological than philosophic', nor have they any fear that 'theology is picture-thinking and must be transcended'.[2] On the contrary, they are confident that any philosophy which dissolves away the realities of man's personal relationship to God, explaining them to be the way in which something else appears to finite minds, stands self-condemned as failing in philosophy's first task, which is to interpret the actualities of our experience without ignoring, distorting or explaining any of them away.

[1] P. F. Chambers, *A Little Book of Baron von Hügel*, p. 31.
[2] W. Moberly, *op. cit.* p. 489.

The change that has come about may be illustrated by reference to the subject of angels. Twenty-five or thirty years ago this was a subject of great difficulty to me and my contemporaries. When theology was under suspicion of being picture-thinking, when the religious idea of God was suspected of being a personification of the spirit of evolutionary process, somewhat after the manner of Britannia or Uncle Sam, of what were the members of the angelic host to be thought of as personifications? How could we preach Michaelmas sermons that would both be honest with ourselves and helpful to our congregations? Some six or seven years ago I suddenly realized that that difficulty had disappeared. If the ultimate reality be the living, active, personal God, Father, Son and Spirit, whose sovereign will has called into existence that fundamental stream of energy which constitutes the time-space universe, if all impersonal things, forces and natural laws be created by Him to be the matrix through which He brings into being us finite human persons, why should it be thought mythological or naïve picture-thinking to believe that He has created other finite, personal spirits and given them also a relative independence and freedom? Once we disabuse our minds of the notion that the more we dissolve away ('transcend' is the philosophic term!) concrete personal self-consciousness the nearer we approach the essence of reality, once we grasp the truth that there is nothing more real than the intensely personal life of the Blessed Trinity, then the thought of angels as forming the natural *entourage* of God in Heaven becomes more reasonable than alternative speculations.

My first point, then, is that present-day theological thought asserts the Christian doctrine of creation in the full sense of the word. The name 'God' is not a personification of the impersonal spirit of a process in space and time; it denotes the living, active, personal Being whose will has called into existence the created universe, who gives it its spatio-temporal reality, a gift including a relative independence and freedom. To think of Him as standing over against His created universe as its sovereign Creator, Sustainer, Ruler, Redeemer and Judge is not a form of naïvely mythological picture-thinking which for philosophical accuracy needs to be replaced by some less concretely personal schematization. On the contrary, it expresses what for philosophy, as well as for religion and theology, is true insight into the ultimate nature of reality.

II

I want next to call your attention to another feature of the past twenty-five years, the recovery of what is sometimes called 'biblical theology'. I can best

explain what is meant by this phrase by the following
quotation from an article published this summer:

Theologians in the nineteenth century were rather
self-consciously on the defensive, rather apt to look
at the Scriptures through nineteenth-century spectacles, and to interpret them in terms of nineteenth-
century ideas, with the result that the historical
criticism of the Bible tended to take the place of
really biblical theology. What has happened since
the last war is that theologians have recovered their
confidence in the Scriptures themselves, recovered
their sense of them as being indeed the Word of
God to man, and not just the record of man's
experience of God.[1]

There is some looseness of expression in this statement, which we must examine if we are to understand
just what has happened. What, for example, is meant
by saying that the vogue of historical criticism was
due to looking at the Scriptures through nineteenth-
century spectacles and interpreting them in terms of
nineteenth-century ideas? As the words stand, they
might mean that the nineteenth century had the
arrogance to sit in judgement on the Bible instead of
asking to be judged by it, an arrogance from which,
presumably, the twentieth century is free. But such
an interpretation would be no less arrogant: why
should we assume that our twentieth-century spec-

[1] R. Cant, in the *Church Quarterly Review*, July–September, 1946,
p. 161.

tacles and ideas are so superior? That cannot be the meaning of this passage. What then? Look back a little further. Before the rise of modern literary and historical criticism our ancestors accepted the Bible as the Word of God in a way which involved accepting every statement in it as divinely guaranteed truth. If the Bible said that the world was created in seven days, or that Jonah spent three days and three nights in the whale's belly, those statements were above criticism. When in the nineteenth century that way of accepting the Bible was challenged by the progress of scientific and historical enquiries, the challenge had to be met, and the only honest way in which the Church could meet it was by encouraging its theologians themselves to subject the Bible to the most rigorous criticism. This had to be done, and we to-day owe a debt of gratitude to those of our forefathers who had faith enough to do it. We should not think of looking through nineteenth-century spectacles as the outlook of arrogant men sitting in judgement on the Word of God. We should think of those scholars as men upon whom the circumstances of their time laid the intolerable strain of finding that what they had taken to be the foundation of their faith was full of quicksands, as men who had faith and courage enough to dig and sift until they secured the solid ground on which they could and we can stand. For the time being this digging and sifting was a whole time job. If they could not be expounding the Bible as the Word of God, that was because they were occupied in making it possible for us to do so.

Again, there is danger of looseness of thought in the suggestion of an antithesis between the Scriptures as the Word of God to man and as the record of man's experience of God. It might lead one to suppose that they must be either one or the other, whereas if they are the first they must necessarily also be the second. For man lives in time, and any record of God making known His Word through His dealings with men inevitably records man's experience of God. It would, I think, be true to say that those nineteenth-century critics concentrated on that aspect of Bible study which deals with the history of man's reception of God's self-disclosure. This was the first bit of solid ground that they found as they dug and sifted, and it is the ground on which we must build to-day if what we call our biblical theology is to have secure foundations. Building on it we arrive at the view of revelation through the Bible which I have described elsewhere as follows:

The eyes of the biblical writers were opened to see the significance of certain events as the key-feature for the understanding of the universe. They proclaim that these events manifest God's redemptive activity, and by surveying the universe from this standpoint they are enabled to recognize elsewhere His creative and preservative activity. The Bible comes to us in the form of propositions because only by statements in the form of propositions could those whose eyes were opened bear record to future generations of what they saw. It is not these propositions as such which are the *revelatum*. They bear record to the *revelatum*, but as the ages go by they can only continue to mediate the revelation in so far as in each generation men's eyes are opened to see for themselves the significance of the revelatory acts of God to which they bear witness.[1]

This view of God's self-revelation through the Bible gives us a foundation for biblical theology which is in keeping with our recovery of belief in the sovereignty of God. Behind everything is the conscious personal activity of the living God. As Creator and Redeemer He is active in the events of this world's history. He is also active in the *testimonium Spiritus Sancti internum* through which prophets and apostles recognized and wrote of what they saw, through which hearers and readers have their minds opened to receive the revelation.

The main purpose of this lecture is to urge the necessity of holding together these two recovered insights which have come to theologians of our time. I have been moved to take this subject because I have noticed in some quarters among enthusiastic advo-

[1] *The Doctrine of the Trinity*, p. 35.

cates of biblical theology a tendency to put it forward in a way which ignores the sovereignty of the living God. The Bible is treated as though it were itself the ultimate source of revealed truth. Those who attempt to explain what they have learned from the Bible through studying it in the light of contemporary scholarship or scientific research are condemned on the ground that, instead of letting God's Word speak for itself and submitting to its judgement, they corrupt and obscure its message by passing it through the distorting medium of fallible human thought. The Bible, it is said, must be accepted as its own interpreter; the only right method of exposition is to interpret one passage by the light of another.

Here we are face to face with a subject of great difficulty. We cannot simply dismiss as groundless the suspicion that men may distort the biblical revelation by reading into it inadequate and possibly erroneous ideas that reflect the spirit of a passing age. This has been done too often for us to be able to shut our eyes to the danger of it. But neither can we shut our eyes to the fact that all honest seeking after truth, whether it be through historical enquiry, through philosophical analysis or through scientific research, is inspired by God, and insights gained through it may be, for their day and generation, *testimonium Spiritus Sancti internum*.

In the world of philosophy it is a commonplace that the weak spot in a system of thought often lies in its uncriticized presuppositions. I am reminded of this whenever I ask myself what can be the ground of the assumption that the Bible itself, by itself, must be the sole and all-sufficient source of theology. Is it more than an induction from the many instances in which the hearing or reading of the Bible has spoken home to the heart of man with self-authenticating authority? That this has happened, and does happen, is evidenced beyond question, and it is psychologically natural that those to whom the Word of God has come in this way should jump to the conclusion that the Bible is for man the sole source of theological enlightenment. What I want to suggest is that the empirical facts on which the conclusion is based are adequately accounted for if, instead of saying that the Bible speaks home to man, we say that God speaks to man through the Bible. When we put it like this, we grasp the corollary that we cannot *a priori* deny to God the power and the right to use other channels of revelation as well. The admirable catholic maxim, *Deus non alligatur sacramentis*, needs to be matched by a parallel evangelical maxim, *Deus non alligatur litera scripta*. Man may be bound to accept the biblical revelation, but God is free to supplement it as He will.

Yet there must be some sense in which we may

believe that God is bound by the biblical revelation. We must not misconstrue God's sovereign freedom as though it meant freedom to contradict Himself. We get the necessary element of fixedness, of *depositum fidei*, when we think of God as having revealed Himself in action, of the Bible as bearing witness to those events in which God put forth His sovereign power within the history of this world for the redemption of His creation from evil. It is as true for the Christian theologian as it was for the ancient Greek poet that

μόνου γὰρ αὐτοῦ καὶ θεὸς στερίσκεται
ἀγένητα ποιεῖν ἄσσ' ἂν ᾖ πεπραγμένα.[1]

What God has done He has done; the proclamation of what He has done has been, and is, and always will be the Christian gospel. As Whitehead has put it: 'The Buddha gave his doctrine to enlighten the world: Christ gave his life. It is for Christians to discern the doctrine.'[2]

'It is for Christians to discern the doctrine.' This reminds us that the Bible is not a bare record of events. It is the record of those events as borne witness to by men whose eyes were opened to see their significance as acts of God. And, as I have said, their witness continues to mediate the revelation to those in each generation whose eyes are similarly

[1] Agathon, quoted in Aristotle, *Eth. Nic.* 1139b.
[2] *Religion in the Making* (New York, 1926), p. 56.

opened to see the significance of what they wrote. The sovereign God is His own interpreter as the *testimonium Spiritus Sancti internum* interprets the message of 'the Holy Ghost...who spake by the prophets'.

We have to recognize the *testimonium Spiritus Sancti internum* both in the insights of piety and the judgements of responsible scholarship, insights and judgements which should be sensitive to God's self-revelation through the arts and sciences. And now there is a further factor to be taken into consideration: the Church. Realization of the importance of the Church might indeed be set alongside of emphasis on the sovereignty of God and biblical theology as a third characteristic of the thought of the past twenty-five years. One can trace its growing prominence in the study programmes of the Oecumenical Movement, and I should like here to pay tribute to the contribution made by your own Principal through the publication in 1938 of his book *Jesus and His Church*. In the immediate context of my last few paragraphs the Church is of importance as an organ of revelation: in the interpretation of Scripture aberrations of individual piety or scholarship may be checked by reference to the corporate witness of the whole Spirit-guided body. But the importance of the Church is not exhausted in its function as in this sense an organ of revelation.

It is itself part of the revelation. Its constitution as the new Israel, its commissioning as the earthly body of the risen Christ through whose members He carries on His work in this world's history, these are among those acts of God to which the Bible bears witness. In Dr Flew's words, 'The Church is in the first place the object of the divine activity, and then the organ or instrument of God's saving purpose for mankind.'[1] What Dr Flew was here urging about the Church was taken for granted five years later when Mr A. M. Hunter published his brief exposition of New Testament teaching.[2] Surveying Christendom as a whole we see that God, the Bible and the Church are the focal points of live interest in the field of theology.

III

'In the beginning God.' I come now to my last point, which is the significance for the Oecumenical Movement of our recovered conviction of the sovereignty of God. I want to suggest that in the field of faith and order what we need for growth in mutual understanding is a deeper realization of what this conviction implies. In 1 Peter i. 22, we are told that in order to grow without hypocrisy in the love of our brethren we must make a strenuous[3] effort

[1] *Op. cit.* p. 33.
[2] *The Unity of the New Testament* (S.C.M. Press, 1943).
[3] ἐκτενῶς.

to let the truth we have accepted with our minds take possession of our feelings and will. Let us try to see what this will mean when the brethren are brethren separated by the present divisions among Christians and the truth is the truth of the sovereignty of God.

We have seen that God works among men through these instruments, the Bible, the Church and the *testimonium Spiritus Sancti internum*. For the moment we will ignore the application of this last phrase to the *consensus fidelium* and think of it simply as referring to the individual conscience. Taking it in this way, I want to put the question, How far are we divided by treating these three, the Bible, the Church and the individual conscience, as ultimates, forgetting that behind them stands the living God who works through them all as His instruments?

Without going outside the communion to which I belong, I have found in some circles a tendency to set the Bible and the Church in opposition, as though they were rival authorities between which a man must choose, to one or other of which he must pledge his allegiance. Some of my friends are never tired of insisting that the Church is founded on the Bible; it derives its claim to be the Church from the Bible in much the same way as a municipality or a college may derive its claim to its possessions or its authority from some title-deeds, charters or statutes. This is to make the Bible the starting point, and carried to its logical conclusion it leads to the fundamentalist type of biblical theology which I have criticized earlier in this lecture. Its *reductio ad absurdum* may be seen in the publications of the British Israelites, where the Bible shares with the Great Pyramid in having the same kind of ultimate authority that a lawyer ascribes to an Act of Parliament. Others of my friends are equally tireless in insisting that the Church is prior to the Bible. The Bible, it is said, is written from faith to faith, and the faith from which it is written is that of the Church. The Church of the Old Covenant produced the books of the Old Testament and determined its canon; the New Israel took this over from the Old as part of its inheritance and added to it the canon of the New Testament. Under the guidance of the Holy Spirit the Church was the author of the Bible, and is therefore its authoritative expositor. To be rightly understood the Bible must be read in the light of the traditions of the Church. The nemesis of this point of view is a tendency to seek to solve every question that may arise by reference to precedents in the past, forgetting that the maxim *quod ubique, quod semper, quod ab omnibus* must include reference to the insights of piety and scholarship in the present and the future. Here steps in a third group, saying that the primary authority must be ascribed to the *testimonium Spiritus Sancti internum.* This may be found exemplified in some so-called modernists in all communions, but perhaps the clearest instances are to be found among Quakers and Unitarians. When I was in the United States in 1943 I learned that one section of the Friends in that country had adopted as its underlying principle the supreme authority of the 'inner light' of the individual, so much so that in that traditionally pacifist Society a Quaker could be an active combatant in the war without losing, or even impairing, his good standing as a Friend. And I remember reading of a Unitarian minister who preached the doctrine of the Trinity by way of championing what he held to be the fundamental principle of unitarianism, individual freedom of thought.

My contention to-day is that to make any one of these three, the Bible, the Church or the inner light, our final and absolute authority is to land ourselves in absurdity, and that in so far as the Church is divided into rival partisans of one or other, it stultifies itself. We have thought of these past twenty-five years as the period in which we have learned that when we say 'God' we do not mean the spirit of the evolutionary process. He is the Creator to whose sovereign will that process owes its existence, in whose sustaining, redeeming and fostering care lies its hope of perfection. It is a poor thing to have emancipated our conception of God from constriction by what we call laws of nature only to re-enslave Him in our minds to the written word, the ecclesiastical institution or the private judgement of individual human beings. We must think of Him as standing behind them and working through all three, using their very tensions and conflicts in order that by their interaction He may lead us onward into fuller knowledge of Himself and conformity to His will. It is by these tensions and conflicts that He keeps our minds alive and moving. It is not His will that once and for all we should settle the general question of priority between the Bible, the Church and the inner light and then put it comfortably out of our minds. His purpose in the creation of man is not to surround Himself in Heaven with the type of functionary whose mind can only be held together by red tape. On the contrary. He has so arranged things that the question we always have to ask, and have to ask over and over again as times and circumstances change, is this: On this occasion, in respect of the issue now before us, where is for us here and now the word of God? Is it to be found in the *prima facie* meaning of the text of Scripture, in the tradition of the Church, in the conscience of contemporary piety, or in the judgement of current scholarship?

Why do we shrink from accepting this as the condition of our earthly pilgrimage? At bottom, if we think it out, we shall find that it is because of the inadequacy of our faith in God. Amid the changes and chances of our earthly life we seek in our religion for something firm and dependable to which we can cling and we do not really put our trust in the living God. We do not believe He can be trusted unless we think of Him as bound by the text of a written document or the tradition of an ecclesiastical body, the conscience of a holy man or the opinion of some theological professors. But this is to seek to find our final and absolute authority within the framework of creation instead of where alone it is truly to be found, in the free sovereign will of the Creator.

Let my last word, then, be this. If we are fully to enter into and profit by that recovery of belief in the sovereignty of God which has been given to us in these last twenty-five years, it must be by a resolute faith in nothing less than God Himself, a faith which, while it strives upward and onward seeking to keep abreast of truth, takes its stand upon the conviction that

> '...behind the dim unknown
> Standeth God within the shadow,
> Keeping watch above his own.'